Vincent van Gogh

Why does it look so swirly?

I thought it was my eyes!

BY LINDA CERNAK • ILLUSTRATED BY J.T. MORROW

Published by The Child's World®
1980 Lookout Drive • Mankato, MN 56003-1705
800-599-READ • www.childsworld.com

Acknowledgments
The Child's World®: Mary Berendes, Publishing Director
Red Line Editorial: Editorial direction and production
The Design Lab: Design

Photographs ©: Vincent van Gogh, cover, 1, 5, 7, 9, 10, 13,
14, 17, 18, 19; Red Line Editorial, 12; Alexander Burkatovski/
Corbis, 21

ISBN 9781626873551
LCCN 2014930694

Printed in the United States of America
Mankato, MN
July, 2014
PA02223

ABOUT THE AUTHOR

Linda Cernak has more than 35 years of experience as a freelance writer and in-house editor of children's classroom readers and student textbooks. Since 1994, Cernak has published numerous children's books in the subject areas of social studies, science, and the arts. In her spare time, Cernak enjoys painting, drawing, and creating stained glass sculptures.

ABOUT THE ILLUSTRATOR

J.T. Morrow has worked as a freelance illustrator for more than 25 years and has won several awards. His work has appeared in advertisements, on packaging, in magazines, and in books. He lives near San Francisco, California, with his wife and daughter.

CONTENTS

CHAPTER 1

Meeting the Impressionists

The year was 1886. Vincent van Gogh had just arrived in Paris, France. The city bustled with activity. Paris was the center of the Western art world. The artists who lived there had created a new style of art. These artists were called the **Impressionists**. Their style was called Impressionism.

Van Gogh was 33 years old. He had tried many different jobs. But he had only been an artist for a few years. Van Gogh grew up in Holland. But it was in Paris, France, where van Gogh met the Impressionist artists. He learned new things about using color and showing nature. Van Gogh would go on to create his own special style of art.

THE IMPRESSIONIST ARTISTS

The Impressionist artists broke rules artists had followed for a long time. Many of these artists painted outdoors. They liked to paint with bright, bold colors. Some of their paintings looked blurry. They painted the way sunlight fell on objects. This new way of painting was shocking to many people. But the new style would change the way people looked at and thought about art. Impressionist art showed that everyday people and objects could be made beautiful through art.

From the Impressionists, van Gogh learned to incorporate color into his artwork.

Van Gogh's first paintings were dark and sad. In Paris, he studied the Impressionist paintings. Many Impressionist paintings captured a moment in time. They showed people doing everyday things. Van Gogh had never seen paintings like these before. He learned to look at nature. He began to paint bright pictures like the Impressionists.

Van Gogh was an artist for only about ten years. During that time, he spent two years in Paris. Then he went to the town of Arles, France. He drew hundreds of **sketches**. He painted hundreds of pictures. Many of them were **self-portraits**. Van Gogh practiced his style of art in his portraits. Over the years, he painted about 40 of them. His self-portraits show that he was a sad person. But his art was beautiful. He created pieces of art that are still admired today.

Why does it look so swirly?

Van Gogh often looks sad in his self-portraits.

CHAPTER 2

Finding the Right Fit

Vincent van Gogh was born in Holland in 1853. As a young boy, he did not show much interest in art. He was not very interested in school, either. When he was 16 years old, he began to work for his uncle. His uncle was an art dealer, someone who buys and sells art. Van Gogh began to learn much about art. He traveled to many cities to sell art. At first he was happy. But van Gogh was not a good art dealer. He argued with customers. His job as an art dealer ended in 1876.

Van Gogh tried different jobs. He became a teacher. But that did not last very long. He worked in a bookstore. That didn't last long either. Then he decided to become a preacher. He wanted to help poor people. When he was 27 years old, van Gogh began to draw. In 1883, he went to live in a small town in the Netherlands. His early drawings were of farmers and peasants, people who worked in fields. He drew weavers, too. At last van Gogh realized what he wanted to do. He decided to become an artist.

Van Gogh cared about the peasants he painted. He wanted to show how hard they worked. During this time, van Gogh painted his first **masterpiece**. It was called *The Potato Eaters*.

The Potato Eaters, *one of van Gogh's first
masterpieces, is very dark and sad.*

Van Gogh was very close to his brother Theo. Theo was also an art dealer. He wanted van Gogh to learn more about art. So van Gogh moved to Paris in 1886. Paris was alive with the Impressionist artists. Van Gogh studied their art. His paintings became bright and cheerful. He became friends with other artists. And he began to create his own style of art. He explored using colors. He tried different brushstrokes. He even put **texture** in his paintings with thick lines of paint.

Seascape at Saintes-Maries *shows the thick texture van Gogh often applied to his paintings.*

Van Gogh stayed in Paris for two years. He lived with Theo. They argued a lot. Soon van Gogh decided to leave Paris. He wanted to paint where it was sunny and bright. So he moved to Arles, France.

PAINTING WITH FEELING

After meeting the Impressionists, van Gogh began painting differently. He used more color. And he painted much more quickly. Sometimes his feelings would take over while he painted. He would squeeze entire tubes of oil paint onto his **canvas**. *Then he would paint with great speed. He wanted to finish his paintings before his feelings or mood left. All of the oil paint created a thick texture on the canvas.*

CHAPTER 3

Experimenting with Color

Van Gogh rented a small house in Arles. Arles is in the south of France. This area is known for its beautiful fields. In Arles, van Gogh experimented with his art. He wanted to use color to show his feelings. Van Gogh painted some of his greatest works in Arles. He painted cheerful pictures of the house. Some paintings were of his bedroom. The paintings

COLOR WHEEL

The color wheel shows how colors go together. They help artists mix colors. There are three **primary colors***. They are red, blue, and yellow. Primary colors cannot be made by mixing other colors. But primary colors can be mixed to make other colors. Orange, purple, and green are mixed from primary colors. For example, mixing red and yellow makes orange. Orange, purple, and green are* **secondary colors***.*

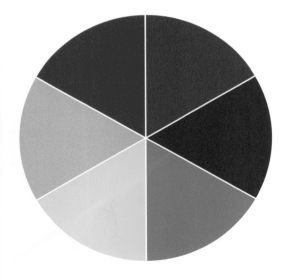

make you feel as if you are in the room. He painted chairs and his cat, too. Van Gogh liked to use opposite colors in his paintings. Opposite colors face each other on the color wheel. Blue and orange are opposite colors. So are yellow and purple. When they are put together, the colors look brighter.

Van Gogh was dazzled by the bright countryside of France. His **landscapes** swirled with color. Van Gogh often painted the same subject over and over. He painted orchards in the springtime. Then he painted the same orchards in winter.

Van Gogh painted dozens of pictures of sunflowers. Some paintings showed the flowers in a vase. A painting like this is called a **still life**. The objects, such as flowers or fruit, are usually set in place by the artist. The sunflowers are some of van Gogh's most famous paintings.

People did not understand van Gogh's paintings. People did not buy his paintings either. Van Gogh had

little money. So his brother Theo sent him money to live on. Van Gogh bought paint and canvases. But sometimes he would run out of money. He often ran out of canvases, too. When this happened, he would just paint over a finished picture.

Van Gogh painted his first name on the vase in his still life painting Vase with Twelve Flowers.

Van Gogh wanted to study and paint with other artists. In 1888, the artist Paul Gauguin came to Arles. Van Gogh invited Gauguin to move in with him. The two artists worked and lived together for two months. They painted many great works and talked about art. But they had different styles of painting. So they argued a lot.

Gauguin only stayed in Arles for two months. One day Van Gogh became very angry with Gauguin. Nobody really knows what happened. Some people think van Gogh tried to attack Gauguin. Gauguin left. He never saw van Gogh again. Van Gogh was very upset. Then he did something very strange. He cut off part of his own ear.

Van Gogh was very sad when Gauguin left. He was sad for a long time. In 1889, he went into a hospital for people with mental illnesses. He stayed there for about one year. While he was in the hospital, van Gogh painted some of his greatest works. Some of them are of the room he stayed in. Some show the view he could see outside his room's window. After staying a while at the hospital, van Gogh was allowed to venture outside of the hospital. Wheat fields and cypress trees filled his canvases. He painted irises, too. One beautiful painting is called *Starry Night*.

The colors in *Starry Night* *swirl with feeling.*

CHAPTER 4

Living On through Art

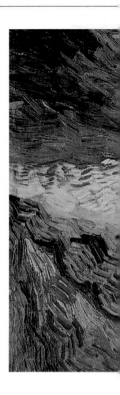

Van Gogh left the south of France in May 1890. He went to a little town outside of Paris. It was called Auvers-sur-Oise. Van Gogh painted away. He worked fast, painting one picture every day. This went on for two months. He painted portraits. He painted the colorful town and church of

Van Gogh painted The Church at Auvers-sur-Oise *in June 1890, just one month before ending his life.*

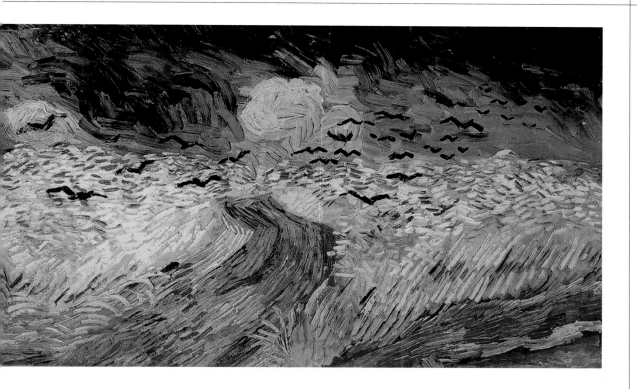

Auvers. Sadly, these would be the last months of van Gogh's life. He wrote letters to his brother Theo and confided in him. But van Gogh was a very sad man. He simply could not find a way to be happy.

One day in July 1890, van Gogh could not take being sad anymore. He ended his life. Even though van Gogh was a sad person, he filled his paintings with beautiful feeling. Many people believe van Gogh's last painting was of a wheat field. Crows fly above the wheat in the painting. The sky is dark and gloomy. It is different from his other paintings. But the wheat field is still bright and yellow.

Wheat Field with Crows *is believed to be van Gogh's last painting.*

After van Gogh died, his brother Theo was very sad. But Theo got all of van Gogh's works. Soon people began to buy van Gogh's paintings. People noticed what a wonderful artist he was. Theo died six months after van Gogh. He passed the paintings on to his family. Years later, the people of Holland built a museum. It opened in 1973. It is filled with van Gogh's works. People come from all over the world. They want to see the beautiful art of van Gogh.

It is believed that van Gogh only sold one painting during his lifetime. It is called *The Red Vineyard*. Today, you can see it in a museum in Russia. Now, Van Gogh's paintings sell for millions of dollars at art auctions. One painting of a wheat field sold for $57 million. It was one of the highest prices ever paid for a painting. It is sad that van Gogh did not live to see how people love his art. Today, people realize how special van Gogh's works are. He is one of the most famous artists of all time.

ART AUCTION

Art lovers have bought some of van Gogh's paintings at art auctions. At an art auction, people offer money for a painting. This is called a bid. People bid on the paintings they like the best. If more than one person keeps bidding, the price goes higher and higher. The person with the highest bid gets the painting. Many of van Gogh's paintings have been sold at art auctions.

Van Gogh's The Red Vineyard *is one of the most valuable paintings in the world.*

Glossary

canvas (KAN-vuhs) A canvas is a heavy cloth on which a painting is made. If van Gogh did not have a fresh canvas to paint on, he painted over a finished painting.

Impressionists (im-PRESH-uhn-ists) Impressionists were French painters of the late 1800s who formed a new style of art. Van Gogh learned new techniques from the Impressionists, such as the use of bright colors.

landscapes (LAND-skapes) Landscapes are large areas of land that can be seen in one view. Van Gogh painted many landscapes showing wheat fields.

masterpiece (MAS-tur-pees) A masterpiece is an artwork of great excellence. *Starry Night* is a masterpiece.

primary colors (PRYE-mair-ee KUHL-urz) Red, blue, and yellow are the three primary colors. Primary colors are mixed to make all other colors.

secondary colors (SEK-uhn-dare-ee KUHL-urz) Secondary colors are made by mixing primary colors. Orange, purple, and green are secondary colors.

self-portraits (self POR-trits) Self-portraits are paintings or drawings a person creates of himself or herself. Van Gogh painted about 40 self-portraits.

sketches (SKECH-us) Sketches are rough or beginning drawings. In addition to his paintings, van Gogh created hundreds of sketches.

still life (STIL LIFE) A still life is a painting or drawing of objects an artist arranges. Van Gogh created many still life paintings of flowers in vases.

texture (TEKS-chur) Texture is the way something feels to the touch. Some of van Gogh's paintings had a bumpy texture because of the gobs of paint he applied to them.

To Learn More

BOOKS

Sabbeth, Carol. *Van Gogh and the Post-Impressionists for Kids: Their Lives and Ideas, 21 Activities.* Chicago: Chicago Review Press, 2011.

Whiting, Jim. *Vincent van Gogh*. Hockessin, DE: Mitchell Lane Publishers, 2008.

Wood, Alix. *Vincent van Gogh*. New York: Windmill Books, 2013.

WEB SITES

Visit our Web site for links about Vincent van Gogh:
childsworld.com/links

Note to Parents, Teachers, and Librarians:
We routinely verify our Web links to make sure they are safe and active sites. So encourage your readers to check them out!

Index